HOW TO SPEAK CHIMPANZEE

A phrasebook of useful
everyday expressions in
Chimpanzee that no human
should be without

Richard Brassey

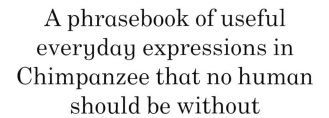

For George
I told you
I knew how

With thanks to Jim Cronin
and all at Monkey World Chimpanzee Rescue Centre,
Wool, Dorset for their help and advice

Published in paperback in 1996

First published in Great Britain in 1995
by Orion Children's Books
a division of the Orion Publishing Group Ltd
Orion House
5 Upper St Martin's Lane
London WC2H 9EA

A catalogue record for this book is available from the British Library
Printed in Italy

The chimpanzee is our closest living relative in the animal kingdom, and chimps have things to say to each other just like we do. But the chimp's tongue and throat are not suited to speaking, so chimps hoot and grunt and make faces and gestures instead.

These are just a few of the ways that chimps tell each other things. There is much of their language that we still do not understand.

Several people have tried to teach chimps human speech. Although they cannot manage this, they can be taught sign language. One famous chimp, named Washoe, not only learnt 130 words in sign language but was able to teach it to other chimps.

This shows how clever chimps are, but learning sign language did not make them happy. They never asked to do it, and, after spending so much time with humans, they found it difficult to get on with other chimps. They have a perfectly good language of their own and they are happiest living in their own family groups.

Like humans, every chimp has its own particular voice and different groups have their own way of saying things, similar to our different accents. Most of the expressions in this book are used by all chimps everywhere.

Soon you will be ready to start speaking Chimpanzee to your family and friends. You'll be amazed at how much they already understand, and you'll be able to teach them the things they don't. When you look in the mirror you'll see that many chimp expressions are the same as yours.

Good morning!

If you are a top chimp, you say good morning by making a lot of noise. You don't hoot or grunt but you shake branches and jump from one branch to another. This wakes up all the other chimps and makes them scream.

Since you yourself probably do not sleep in a tree, you could try jumping on your bed, shaking your bedclothes and running up and downstairs instead. This will make your family scream.

If you are not a top chimp, you can just get up quietly . . . until the top chimp wakes up. Then **you** have to scream!

Does anybody here speak Chimpanzee?

Hooo! her — Hooo! her — Hooo! her!

Put your lips together and give a long hoot – "Hooo!" Breathe
in noisily – "Her!" – and repeat.

Waaa!

You can hoot as many times as you like. When you have finished, if you feel like it, you can sign off by throwing back your head and shouting "Waaa!"

The whole call is known as a PANT HOOT and you answer, "Yes, I speak Chimpanzee," in exactly the same way – "Hooo! her-Hooo! her-Hooo! her . . ." and, if you feel like it, "Waaa!"

This is my house. I live here!

Hoo! her — Hoo! her — Hoo! her!

Choose a tree outside your house. Jump up and down and beat on it with your fists and feet. If you don't have any trees, you can try beating on your front door. While doing this you should PANT HOOT loudly.

This will let any chimps who are around know that it's your neighbourhood.

Hello!
Hu! Hu!

There are many ways of saying hello in Chimp depending on who you are talking to – someone bigger, someone smaller, a good friend, a stranger.

Chimps grunt "Hu! Hu!" They touch, shake hands and even kiss. While kissing they usually pant.

Hi! Can I pick around in your hair?

Smack! Smack! Smack!

Smack your lips together quietly and hold out your hand. This is a very friendly greeting in Chimpanzee.

Chimps spend a lot of time picking through each other's hair. It is something they really enjoy. They pick out any little bits and pieces they find such as dead skin, dirt, leaves or even, very occasionally, a bug.

If you find anything interesting, stop, grunt, smack your lips and maybe pop it in your mouth. If you should happen to find a bug, aim carefully, smack loudly and scrunch it up . . . delicious!

Hi! Will you pick around in my hair?

Clack! Clack! Clack!

This is also a very friendly greeting.

Stick one arm in the air and scratch your armpit vigorously with the other hand. At the same time clack your teeth together.

If your friend starts to lose interest while picking, clack your teeth together loudly to remind him to concentrate – clack! clack! clack!

I'm starving. Gimme!
ough ough ough ough!

Try this on your parents in the kitchen when you're hungry. Stick out your lips in a big pout. Grunt lots of times. Point to what you want and hold out your hand.

It usually works.

I'll die if you don't let me have it!

eee eee eee aah aah aah AAH AAH!

You can try pouting for anything, not just food. Stand by the thing you want and pout until your lips feel as though they are going to fly off your face. You start with a low grunt – "Ough! Ough!" – but bit by bit, if you are not getting what you want, you grunt higher and louder until eventually you are screaming:

"eee eee eee aah aah aah AAH AAH!"

If this doesn't work, it is normal in Chimpanzee to lie down on the floor and go crazy. This is known as a TEMPER TANTRUM.

Come and get some of this!

Aaaa!

Chimps hate sharing their food, but they get so excited when they find something tasty that they just can't help telling everybody.

This high-pitched call is repeated several times from when you see the food until you start eating. You can also smack your lips just thinking about it.

Dee-licious!

Her, hmmm, her

To show something tastes great, look happy and grunt – three short low grunts – "Her, hmmm, her."

If you are really enjoying your food, chew it up until it's mushy, stick it out on the edge of your lower lip and have a good look at it over the end of your nose. This is not considered rude by chimps.

Let's play!

This is called PLAYFACE.

Open your mouth wide and show your lower teeth, being careful to keep your top teeth covered. Showing your top teeth is often a sign of anger.

It may help to point to the thing you want to play with and, if you are human, to brush your teeth first.

This is funny!

Hee huh hee huh hee huh!

Chimps tend to keep PLAYFACE on all the time they are playing.

They laugh in a wheezy, chuckly, high-pitched way – "Hee huh hee huh hee huh!"

This is really crazy!

eee eee ough eee *aah ough aah aah*

AAH AAH!

This face is for when you are overexcited, and is only to be tried on good friends. People who don't know you might think you are angry with them.

Open your mouth wide, scream as loud as you can (short high gargly screams) and leap about.

This is weird!

Hu!

Open your eyes wide. The "Hu!" should be spoken softly just to warn your friends. You don't want to let everybody know you are around.

Look out!

Wraaa!

Scream "Wraaa!" as loud as you can. Your face will take on the right expression automatically.

I'm scared.
eee eee aah aah AAH AAH !

Clamp your teeth together but open your lips very wide and scream. When chimps get scared they hold hands.

Okay, so you never get scared.

I'm so miserable.

Hoo-wha— hoo-hoo

When chimps feel sad, they whimper and cry, although they don't shed tears the way we do.

Sob "hoo," gulp in "wha," and sob again "hoo hoo."

I really like you.

The way to say you really like someone is to hug and kiss them the way we do. Don't forget to pant while you are kissing.

So who do you like that much?

Shhh! I'm thinking.

When chimps are thinking, they look as if they are thinking.

I'm so bored.

You know how to look bored, don't you? So do chimps.

This looks really interesting.

Chimps look interested when they are interested.

Hey you! Back off!

OUGH!! OUGH!! OUGH!! OUGH!!

Open your mouth as wide as you can and show all your teeth. Your hair should also stand on end. Unfortunately most human hair does not stand on end by itself, so you may need hair gel. If this face doesn't work at once, start shouting:

"OUGH!! OUGH!! OUGH!! OUGH!!"

however many times it takes.

This also means "I'M FED UP!" or "I'M SICK OF THIS!"

WARNING: If you try this face on someone who is bigger than you, be ready to run, or see the next two pages.

It's cool, man.

Wah! Wah!

Let your lower lip hang down. Hunch over as though you were bowing. Bounce up and down and bark: "Wah! Wah!"

This tells the others that you don't want to fight.

Just leave me alone, okay.

Clamp your teeth together. Open your lips in a grin. Cover your head with your hands. Pretend you're not really there. (It doesn't always work.)

The grin does not mean you are happy.

I'm in charge around here.

Squeeze your lips together but keep them firmly shut and try to make them meet your eyebrows over your nose. Also make your hair stand on end. (See: Hey you! Back off!)

Once you have got the face right, pull yourself up to your full height. Square your shoulders and run around like crazy banging things, thumping and drumming – the louder the better. This really impresses other chimps. Don't say anything yourself. The idea is to make everybody else scream.

WARNING: YOU HAD BETTER MAKE SURE YOU ARE IN CHARGE BEFORE STARTING. Otherwise sooner or later somebody is going to come along and tell you to shut up.

Goodnight!

Eh mmmmmm

Most chimps go to bed quietly after a busy day, but occasionally they grunt contentedly: "Eh mmmm." This might be a good idea. It will let everybody know that you are resting.